VANILLA ICE

The *hottest* phenomenon to hit
the music charts

"Ice Ice Baby"
the first single by a rapper to top
Billboard's Pop Chart

★

"To the Extreme"
His first album, with more
than four million copies sold

★

"Play That Funky Music"
his second single, which *shipped* platinum

★

Here is the full scoop on the hottest
craze in the music world.

ICE ICE ICE

THE EXTRAORDINARY

VANILLA

ICE

STORY

MARK BEGO

A DELL BOOK

Published by
Dell Publishing
a division of
Bantam Doubleday Dell Publishing Group, Inc.
666 Fifth Avenue
New York, New York 10103

ISBN: 0-440-21013-5

Printed in the United States of America

February 1991

10 9 8 7 6 5 4 3 2 1

OPM

To M.C. Vicki Green.
You're a super def hottie!

———————

The author would like to thank the following people for their help, encouragement, and assistance in completing this book:

John Bush
David Gale
Glenn Hughes
Claire Krane
Ken Lane
Charlene Mills
Marie Morreale
Tommy Quon
Anne Raso
David Salidor
Tony Seidl
Peter Seitz
Barbara Shelley
Sherry Tonkel
Dave Weiner

CONTENTS

INTRODUCTION

In the music world the term "flavor of the month" is frequently used to describe whoever is the Number One artist on the music charts. In 1984 it was Michael Jackson, in 1985 it was Madonna, and the list goes on and on. Now, in late 1990 and early 1991, the Number One artist in America is Vanilla Ice, and critics are trying to peg him with the same limiting labels that are used to topple other pop icons. Yes, like others before him, Ice is experiencing life from the dizzying perspective of being at the top of the heap—but the similarity also extends to his musical scope and his media durability as well. Like Prince, Madonna, Michael Jackson, Mick Jagger, The Beatles, and Cher, Vanilla is destined to become a movie star as well as a recording star. He is out to prove that he is no mere flash-in-the-pan sensation.

Like millions of fans across the country, I first became aware of Vanilla Ice via his infectious Number One hit single, "Ice Ice Baby," and his phenomenally successful tour with M. C. Hammer. When the opportunity arose for me to write about Vanilla Ice, I jumped at the chance. I liked his music, and was genuinely curious about what makes him tick.

While I was working on the book, the infamous Milli Vanilli scandal broke in the newspapers, and like hungry crows in a field of wheat, critics and skeptics began to peck at Vanilla Ice's various press statements about his past. While the controversy about Milli Vanilli concerned their very ability to sing and to perform, there was never any doubt about Ice's talent as a rapper and a dancer. The attacks concerned three factual topics: (1) the high school he attended, (2) the misunderstanding about which Motocross contests he raced in, and (3) what his real name and hometown were. As bad publicity often does, it only fanned the blazing flame of Vanilla Ice's popularity. The week that the press stories broke on the Ice controversy, Vanilla's debut SBK Records album "To the Extreme" didn't drop from the number one slot; instead it sold about an extra million copies! In addition, "Ice Ice Baby" has become a huge hit in England, Germany, and Australia as well.

As an investigative reporter, I have written this book in an attempt to shed light on the reasons for the misleading facts and to discover the truth about this instantaneously accepted new music star. Unlike other "at-face-value" artists, there is an element of mystery and even provocativeness about Vanilla Ice. The important facts, however, do not concern what high school he actually attended or what neighborhood he grew up in. The real issues that are fascinating concern how a white boy from the suburbs of Miami and Dallas could excel at the predominantly black art form of rap music and masterfully capture the respect of both black and white audiences alike.

What is Vanilla Ice like? I find him to be a fascinating subject to write about. He exudes a genuine enthusiasm for the tornado of excitement that he has caused in the entertainment world. While some media stars immediately shun fans and the press the minute they become big, Ice expresses a devoted passion for being understood by his fans and by the media.

Vanilla seems to be genuinely hurt by the treatment that he has received from newspapers and publications like *People* magazine. Not that he unrealistically expects to be liked and praised by everyone who hears his music, but he found himself beginning to be attacked with a vengeance by the press. In this book, I explore two Vanilla Ices—the one who is a superconfident media star and the one who seems still in awe of the overwhelming reception his music has received in so short a time. Here, for the first time, is the whole Vanilla Ice story, from the controversial stories of his past to the shining glory of his multi-platinum million-selling present. This is Ice, Ice, Ice.

THE ICEMAN COMETH

Yo, listen up: there's a new kid on the block, bustin' a rhyme, and makin' that climb—to the top of the charts. When he's hot—he's smokin' and sizzlin', when he's cold—he's def and chillin'. His jams are fresh, his look is fly. He's tourin' the globe—makin' the rounds, spreadin' the sound he calls "aboveground." Since he arrived on the scene he's been in favor, provin' that he's no mere monthly flavor. He's the hottest thing—there is no maybe, with his platinum single—"Ice Ice Baby." This homeboy is one fresh slice, known around the globe as Vanilla Ice.

Raised in the slick sun capital of Miami, and

initially bustin' loose from a club called City Lights in Dallas, Vanilla Ice is the first bona fide recording star of the nineties. Burning white hot and picking up new fans in a frenzy, Ice is not only the first rap artist to hit Number One on America's pop single chart, but on the pop album chart as well. Ten weeks after its release, the Vanilla Ice LP, ''To the Extreme'' sold four million copies and catapulted him over the top. Oddly enough, by reaching Number One, Vanilla's album broke M. C. Hammer's twenty-one-week stranglehold on the top slot with his LP ''Please Hammer Don't Hurt 'Em.'' Not only is Hammer the Iceman's top competitor in the rap market, but he was recently his touring mate on the deffest concert bill of the decade—which also features the sexy female group En Vogue. Since then Ice has embarked on his own phenomenal head-lining tour.

According to Ice, ''For almost six months, Hammer was Number One singing 'you can't touch this'—well, I touched it.'' Instead of looking upon his position on their tour together as that of ''opening act,'' the ever-competitive Vanilla has his own unique perspective. ''Hammer's closing for me—for real!'' he claimed at the time. ''We're turning it out wherever we go—the crowd is coming for me, not him. . . . I mean, I'm not trying to sound like I've got a big head or anything, but he's going to have to take a backseat to the Iceman." One might be tempted to say, "Please Vanilla, Don't Hurt Him!"

In a business where attitude is everything, Vanilla has "cool" to spare. Looking like a combination of Dolph Lundgren and a hip-hop Max Headroom, he cuts a mean profile. With his chiseled cheekbones, and trademark brown-with-a-streak-of-white straight-in-the-air hair, Vanilla is an unmistakable original. Together with the Beastie Boys and Third Base, Ice is one of the only white artists in the almost exclusively black art form of rap. However, like Hammer, the Iceman has found Top Ten appeal with black and white artists alike. How does the subject of breaking the color barrier affect him? "I have to work twice as hard to get over," he admits, "because I am white in an all-black market." Ice claims that you have to gain people's respect for an all-black crowd to accept a white man rapping. "I'd say ten percent of the people think I'm black, and when I come out [onstage] it's like, 'Wow!' But it really hasn't been a problem."

In fact, Vanilla is the first to dispel any thoughts that there is any racial issue involved in the success or failure of a rap artist. Ice explained, "Hammer sold over six million rap albums and made it really commercial. He's black. My album has sold over four million so far, and I'm white. There's no racial thing in rap at all."

On the surface, to look at the facts and figures, one might immediately think of Vanilla Ice as an "overnight success" story. Yes, his fame has been almost instantaneous, but like all new-on-the-scene acts, the immediate onslaught of fame and fortune merely represents the tip of this man's iceberg. In reality, Ice and his performing troupe, the Vanilla Ice Posse (V.I.P.), have been working toward this for quite some time. They have been performing for three years but just recently have received national recognition. "I think it's because I'm real, one hundred percent," he stresses. He feels that the audience can tell by his raps that they are authentic and straight from the streets.

The streets of Miami and Dallas are where he's from, so you know that Ice speaks the stone cold truth. All of the songs on Vanilla Ice's debut album were written by him in collaboration with members of his posse. They reflect his feelings and his life experiences, with life, love, and the pursuit of the endless groove. Ice says that writing rap is no different from writing other music. He has said that "Rap is getting very sophisticated. It's more musical," not only a "beatbox and anything that rhymes anymore." He also claims that story lines have gotten more "intricate." He explains, "My style is such that I put all of my rhymes into a story form, and you can understand every single word I say. You can make a movie out of every song on the album."

Speaking of movies, Vanilla Ice has wasted no time doing his movie star turn. While his "To the Extreme" was busy catapulting its way to the top of the stack, Vanilla was already in front of the cameras working on his major motion picture screen debut. His appearance in the forthcoming *Teenage Mutant Ninja Turtles II: The Secret of the Ooze* is one of 1991's most anticipated releases. Not only does he appear in the film, he also wrote—in collaboration with his deejay, Earthquake—and performed the theme song, which they recently completed in Canada. He has indicated that he would like to get into acting in the future. "I could play a villain, but right now I think that image would lose album sales for me." Ice has nothing to worry about in that department, as it seems that he can do no wrong.

To listen to the lyrics on Ice's "To the Extreme" album, one would think that this twenty-two-year-old five-foot-eleven rap star extraordinaire is one nonstop sex machine. According to him, he has learned that there is more to life at the top than one long endless party. While he enjoys and appreciates his sizzling tidal wave of success, he realizes how much hard work is involved. People may think that it is all girls and a lot of money, but actually to get to the top and stay there, a performer must devote an extraordinary amount of time and effort to his work. As Ice has admitted, "I bust a sweat the first second I hit the stage!"

Unbridled adulation has its price, and now that he is a mega-star, the way he is perceived by fans has changed. "They seem to go crazy all the time," he says of the girls who "bust a move" whenever he is in sight. Girls sometimes grab him, and one fainted in the elevator when she realized she was standing near him. Other fans have sent him nude photos. Although Ice would like people to consider him as just a normal person, his fans still go wild. He has said they even "write about nasty sexual things they'd like to do to me that even I couldn't think of." The fact is, however, when Ice is not performing on the road, he uses his spare time to sleep.

To what does Vanilla attribute his phenomenal success? According to him, it's his lyrics, and the honesty that flows through them, since he writes or cowrites all of his own lyrics. Unlike some other rappers, his lyrics do not seem to offend people. Since his lyrics are clean and contain no curse words, he calls his rap "aboveground." According to him, when you buy a Vanilla Ice record, you get Vanilla Ice, not some nameless producer as with some other performers. As Ice has explained it, to be an artist, "you have to have your own personality." As a homeboy with a solid heart, Vanilla Ice has personality to spare. He has a warm nature and a stone-cold sincerity to back it up.

Rap is a business where originality counts heavily. Too many rappers, lacking originality, try to imitate established performers, and Vanilla Ice feels that this is a big mistake. He considers the elements of the best rap music to be a strong story, a good beat, and a sound that is innovative. His style is more sophisticated than many other rappers. Not only is Ice's rap very musical, but he strives to make his lyrics easy to understand on records and in concert. He has recognized that rap requires more live instruments and fewer prerecorded tracks.

Will success spoil Vanilla Ice? It hasn't so far. He says he is the "same person" he was before his rise to fame, even though the way he lives has undergone a complete change. He has suddenly found that people who weren't friendly before "are now trying to be my best pals." That is what he says he was referring to in his song "Play That Funky Music." Listen to it closely, and you'll understand his message about his ability to "cure" his audience like a rapping witch doctor.

Not only is Vanilla Ice reaping the accolades of his fans, but he is also highly respected among other rap stars as well. Vanilla Ice met Luther Campbell of the group 2 Live Crew at a music convention a few months ago. Campbell told Ice that he admired his music. Although Ice acted calm in front of Campbell, he claims that he "screamed for joy" once he left the building. This was a turning point: acceptance as a rap artist by someone of Campbell's caliber.

What is it that makes rap so hot? Vanilla says that rap's appeal is due to the bass, which makes it good dance music. He has referred to it as "the music of the ghetto." While rap is highly derivative of rock, R&B, and dance music, it is something uniquely all its own—it's like brutally fresh urban poetry. Rap has been around for ten years, but it has been a slow craze to catch on, as not everyone is into the sound of rap. Although some people consider rap to be the worst popular music since disco, Ice quickly retorts, "Let me tell you something—no music will ever be worse than disco!"

Not only has Vanilla Ice been all over the airwaves with "Ice Ice Baby" and the follow-up single, "Play That Funky Music," but television has also jumped into the act. His videos have been in "heavy rotation" on *Yo! MTV Raps*, *Soul Beat*, *Hit Video USA*, *Video Jukebox*, and a myriad of other video shows. He has been a guest video jockey on MTV, he's been featured on *Entertainment Tonight*, appeared live on *Club MTV*, and rapped on *Arsenio Hall*. By December 1990, Ice had already been featured in *People*, *Time*, *Teen Machine*, and *Teen Dreams* magazines and been photographed for the covers of *Hits* and *Rolling Stone* magazines—and the media blitz has just begun!

Before he hooked up with the M. C. Hammer tour, Vanilla Ice shared the same stage with a veritable "who's who" of rap. Among the acts he has been on the bill with are Paula Abdul, NWA, Rob Base, Tone Loc, EPMD, Sir Mix-A-Lot, and Public Enemy.

To view all of these successful aspects of Ice's past year of international fame, it could appear that his life has been a charmed one.

However, his glittering stature in 1991 is in direct contrast to his roller coaster early years. Before he was interested in music or in rapping, Vanilla's main passion was racing motorcycles—specifically on the Motocross circuit. He says that he began racing in the Motocross at age six and had thought of becoming a professional racer. Although he loved the thrill of the race, motorcycle accidents were beginning to take a toll on his body. He broke his left ankle three times. Once he broke both ankles, and was told there was a chance that he would never walk again. After two operations and lots of physical therapy, he was able to go from a wheelchair to crutches. Now he has complete movement and can dance as well as he ever could. Although he would love to ride a motorcycle again, he knows that he should not, and he won't do it.

If you've ever seen Vanilla Ice dance onstage or in his videos, you know that what he says is true. His recovery was total and now he can dance circles around his competition.

Although the motorcycle accidents were a tragic obstacle to overcome, nothing quite tops another series of events in the continuing adventures of Vanilla Ice. According to him, as a teenager he got involved in what he refers to—with an air of embarrassment—as "gangs and stuff." He was, as he has described himself, "a kid that grew up in the ghetto," so that a firsthand knowledge of street smarts went with the territory. He says that he lived only a block away from the projects where many of his friends lived. He only narrowly survived that experience, as he recounts in retrospect: being a member of a street gang can be hazardous to one's health. On several occasions he found himself caught between a knife and a rival gang member.

Five times Ice was stabbed, and he almost died. One stabbing four years ago resulted in the loss of four pints of blood, half the blood in most humans. When he recovered he felt as though he had been given "a second chance," and he frequently thanks God for rescuing him from the street gangs.

Because of his experiences with street gangs, at the beginning of his career he refused to divulge his real name. "I'm from the street—that's why I don't give out my name," he explained in *Time* magazine. For Vanilla Ice, his identity was his most closely guarded secret.

Not only is there mystery and intrigue in Ice's personal story about how he made it to the top, there have also been legal controversies as well, which are discussed later in this

15

book. The first controversy arose just as Vanilla's first single, "Ice Ice Baby" was easing its way into the national Top Ten charts. The song itself begins with that infectiously catchy bass line that had people from Tacoma to Tallahassee wondering, "Where have I heard that before?" It is that same masterful bass line, borrowed from David Bowie and Queen's 1981 single, "Under Pressure," that contributed to the success of the single. "Ice Ice Baby" is unlike other rap songs because it has the infectious drive of a rock song, due to that bass line.

As you can see, there are many unanswered questions and a maze of mysterious circumstances surrounding the Vanilla Ice story. How did this white ghetto rapper with the *G.Q.* looks elbow his way to the top in a predominantly black field? What does he have that neither black rappers, like M. C. Hammer— nor white rappers, like The Beastie Boys— have? What originally took him to the rap clubs of Dallas? What was he able to do there that he couldn't accomplish in Miami? And more importantly—how does he get his hair to stand up on end like that? On the surface, he is just a good-looking guy who can rap his heart out in a way that fans—black and white—can all identify with. Yet, on the other side of the coin, there is much more to the Iceman than meets the eye.

Stay chilled, because these are all mere headlines in the fascinating story of the hottest, coldest, deffest, baddest rapper on the scene. The Ice Age has just begun anew. But this time around the jams are def, the look is fly, and the flavor is unmistakably vanilla—*Vanilla Ice*, that is!

2

MIAMI ICE

Generally, when you're dealing with the biography of a famous person who is known by a name other than the one he or she is born with, when it comes time in the book to discuss the childhood and early years of the subject, the biographer will reveal the subject's true identity. Well, Vanilla Ice is a totally different and unique recording star, so the first thing we're going to do is to throw away the rules. No good mystery writer—whether Agatha Christie or Stephen King—would reveal the solution to the mystery too soon in his or her story. Before Vanilla Ice first began hitting America's Top Ten charts, he had successfully kept his identity a closely guarded secret. When his music and his face were suddenly all over the airwaves, it became obvious that his real name and background would eventually surface. Too many people in Florida and Texas knew the real "Iceman."

Growing up in the streets of Miami, Florida, the teenage Ice got involved with several street gangs. According to him, when he became "Vanilla Ice," he felt that he had to make a clean break from the past, and he wants to leave his long-since-forgiven mistakes behind him.

When I began work on this book in November of 1990, one of the first subjects that had to be addressed was the matter of his true identity. Since no one seemed to know who he was, after much thought, I decided to set up the matter of his legal name as one of the many unsolved mysteries about him in this book—until the point in the story where it was leaked by the press.

It had become a big issue in the media. "Miami's getting mad at it because they don't know my real name," said Ice to the press. "They're running contests on the radio, announcing, 'If you went to school with Vanilla Ice, and you know his real name, please call here and tell us.'" It really made everyone crazy because he wouldn't tell anybody where he went to school. He figured that if he divulged the facts, his "cover" would be blown.

In Vanilla Ice's original press bio it mentioned the fact that while in Miami he attended Palmetto High School, alongside Luther Campbell, who is "Luke" of the rap group 2 Live Crew. Actually, Ice attended several schools, including North Miami Beach High School and R. L. Turner High School in Carrolton, Texas, and he met Luther Campbell only recently. This misinformation has helped to deepen the mystery that surrounded Vanilla Ice.

Now that we have resolved that issue, let's go back to Halloween of 1968, because that was the day that Vanilla Ice was born, the second of three children. Most people who are born on holidays lament the fact that the holiday overshadows the celebration of their birthday. Not Vanilla Ice. He thinks that it's great "because that way everyone remembers it." He has stated that it's always been great for him, and that he's happy to have it on a holiday because nobody forgets his birthday, and they usually end up remembering to buy him a present.

Oddly enough, both of Vanilla's siblings were born on holidays too. His brother, who is five years older than Ice, was born on Christmas day. His younger sister was born on Emancipation Day, a Southern holiday.

Keeping to the "mystery" theme of this chapter, one of the other great mysteries of Vanilla Ice's life is the identity of his father. Ice has said he never knew his father, who was not around when Ice was growing up. In fact, he absolutely refuses to talk about him.

In direct contrast, Ice speaks glowingly and frequently of his mother. She's a music teacher who, according to Ice, has taught a number of instruments. According to Ice's manager, Tommy Quon, Ice's mother is a concert pianist. It seems that her love of music was a major influence on Vanilla Ice. However, her interest was in classical music, while Ice was only into the rap scene. While this may not have pleased her at the time, Ice's success may have changed her attitude toward rap music. For Christmas of 1990, Ice fulfilled a long-time dream of being able to buy his mother a grand piano as a present. She was totally blown away by the surprise when her son presented it to her.

According to Vanilla, his mom had to play both mother and father to her three children. Although she encouraged them to go to school and do their homework, she also allowed them to allot their time however they saw fit. She didn't pressure Ice into doing something if he didn't want to.

Ice's family life was hardly the "white bread" existence of *The Brady Bunch*. With regard to the rest of his family tree he claims to be "part Apache. I am also part Cuban, but other than that I'm really not sure."

Although many details about the "who, what, when, where, and why" aspects of Ice's growing-up years were camouflaged to keep his identity guarded, he has revealed that, "Growing up in Florida, I lived in two different areas: in Hialeah, and I lived in Miami Lakes."

It was reported widely in the press that Ice was one of a few white kids living and growing up in a predominantly black neighborhood. Instead of finding it intimidating, he found it stimulating and exciting. "It was great, I loved it," he says, remembering the fun aspects of his childhood. "It's a different way of growing up. I grew up in the streets of the ghetto." He says he lived in a lower middle class area, and one block away from his house were the projects, and all of the kids from the area went to the same school. His whole life was hanging out in the projects and in the streets of the ghetto. That's where all of his friends were from. Most middle-class white kids don't go into the ghetto to hang out, but to Ice it didn't seem like anything out of the ordinary.

Years later Ice was to look back on his childhood and to appreciate its uniqueness. According to him, "Then when everything started happening for me," he realized how different his childhood had been. After he left Florida he would look at the rest of the world and laughingly comment, "These white people really can't dance!" Then he would think about it and realize that maybe it's because they didn't grow up like he did. That's the obvious reason for his natural ability to rap.

Even within his own household, Ice's perception was distinctly individual. He recalls that his brother was different from him and more like any other normal white kid you see every day. His brother was into rock and roll, and Ice would go through his old records and listen to them. One of his brother's records that Ice distinctly remembers liking was the David Bowie and Queen song "Under Pressure."

What was one of Vanilla's best memories of growing up in the Miami area? According to him, it was when he won his first regional championship for Motocross.

Ice got involved with racing motorcycles at Motocross events at an early age. He started when he was about six years old with a small bike about two feet tall with training wheels, called an Indian. He was one of the youngest racers. The age range for the races goes from ten up to twenty-five years old for professional racers. Everyone races on the same track, but there are completely different classes of racers: novice, intermediate, expert, and pro. He rode in all of the various classifications. He also rode pro for three years in national championships. The first year he says he was named "Rookie of the Year" and won a fourth-place title in 1985's Florida Winter National Olympics.

It was actually his brother who originally got him involved in the whole Motocross scene. After his brother got hurt in a motorcycling accident, he wanted Ice to race so that he could still be involved. To accomplish that, Ice's brother acted as his coach at the events. It wasn't long before Ice himself really found himself hooked on the exhilaration of racing.

The racing track for the Motocross event itself, with the big double jumps, triple jumps, and berms, is made of dirt. The starting gate holds approximately forty riders. There are two "Moto's," the scores of which are combined to make an overall total. If a rider places second in the first Moto and first in the second Moto, the racer instantly wins. But if he gets a first in the first Moto and a second in the second Moto, he gets second place. Winning the second Moto gives the racer the edge, but the winner still must place high in the first Moto. It's best to win both of the Moto's. In the pros category, racers can win money, plaques, and trophies. Experts win money alone, and intermediates and novices just win trophies. There is a beginners class as well.

Generally, the Motocross events are raced with 60 cc (engine size) motorcycles, and they are grouped in 60 cc novice, intermediate, and expert classes. There are also 80 cc class motorcycles, known as a "mini-senior" class, which consists of the same novice/intermediate/expert divisions, and then the same classifications with 120 cc and 250 cc motorcycles, plus an "open class" division. The Supercross consists of 250 cc motorcycles. This is for stadium racing.

It seems that Ice was quite a popular rider on the circuit. He raced for Yamaha and for Kawasaki. He says he never had the opportunity to ride for Suzuki. There are different sponsorships from each of these companies, in which they give you bikes and equipment and pay for all of your expenses.

What was it that he liked the most about the Motocross circuit? The thrill of winning. He's a competitor at heart, that's just his personality, which has made him the success he is today.

One of the most helpful advantages to come from Ice's involvement in Motocross was a direct effect it had on his schoolwork. The races helped him to keep going to school, due to the fact that when he began racing with team sponsorship, his grades had to be passing to continue to compete. According to Motocross rules, to sign a contract, racers also have to maintain a certain grade point average.

Although he loved racing, and it was keeping him from quitting school, Ice soon found that there were several perils that went along with the territory. Accidents are one of the dangers of the events, and Ice had several. Finally, one particular mishap on the track signaled the end of his motorcycling career. "I broke one of my ankles in three places," Vanilla has related of one of his accidents. He had some surgery on it, and underwent a lot of physical therapy. Now his legs work better than ever! When he had the operation, the doctor told him that there was an eighty percent chance that he might never be able to walk again. The physical therapy worked, as his flashy dancing will attest. His legs are back to normal again. He claims that he doesn't want to take any chances by getting back on a bike again.

Just looking at Ice's Motocross adventures, and the sense of self-discipline that he gained from them, one would think that his teenage years were all comprised of creative fun. But there was another side of the coin. While the streets of the inner city can seem like an urban playground of pavement and excitement, danger does lurk there, and it wasn't long before the young Iceman found himself deeply embroiled in it, as he would say, "to the extreme."

PLAY THAT FUNKY MUSIC, WHITE BOY

As a teenager Ice and his family moved from Miami to Dallas, and again he found himself hanging out on street corners, hanging out with a tough street-wise crowd. Simultaneous with his involvements in Motocross, young, tough, and impressionable Vanilla Ice found himself involved with notorious gangs in Dallas. Before this tragic series of episodes was over, he would almost lose his life. Looking back on this chapter of his life, Ice is thankful for finding the guidance and strength to turn his life around.

From the perspective of the 1990s, what were the reasons that Ice got involved with the street gangs to begin with? "Maybe it has something to do with not having a father," he surmises. "I really can't say, and answer the question too accurately." But, his not having a father, and his not really having someone to tell him what to do might have something to do with it. Looking back on those years, Ice has become a lot smarter and can understand why he did the things he did. It was because he didn't have anybody to tell him what to do. If he didn't want to go to school, he simply didn't go.

Through all of his involvement with rival gangs, Ice feels that someone was looking out for him and his well-being, and that God was on his side the whole way because he admits that he was uncontrollable. He would leave the house and come back anytime he wanted to. At thirteen and fourteen years old, he would leave anytime he pleased. His mother, Beth Miño, did her best to look after Ice, but with two teenage boys, she had her hands full. Looking back, Ice wishes that he hadn't been rebellious and feels bad about it. That's another reason why he claims he prays to God every day. He tried his mother's patience, like most teenagers do. When kids don't listen to their parents, that's when bad things start happening, Ice has told reporters. "I didn't listen to my parents and that's when bad things started happening. But God sure did straighten me up—God sure did straighten me up quick!"

Ice has related some of his worst memories of life in the streets by saying, "It was when I got stabbed five times!"

Explaining that terrifying event in a press interview, Ice recalled, "It was a *serious* gang fight." He explained, "I was taking up for a friend" who got beat up by another gang. "We actually beat this dude up pretty bad." He recalls that he and his friends were walking back to their nearby car when someone came up from behind him, grabbed Ice, and started stabbing him. Ice didn't even realize that he had been stabbed because it all happened so quickly.

He was exhausted from the fight, and he put his hand on his knee, in order to catch his breath. He felt something wet, and that is when he realized that he had been stabbed. Blood was gushing out of his leg. A main artery in his leg had been cut in both the front and the back. He was also stabbed on the right side of his back, and on the back of the head, where he still has a little scar. "Every time I cut my hair short, there's a little scar on the back of my head where he stabbed me," Ice said. People have only eight pints of blood in their body, and he lost four pints, requiring three blood transfusions. He was lucky that there was a donor.

Looking back on this whole tragic episode, does it seem that it was a different person in Ice's body, doing all of that? "It was," he admits. "It was a completely different person." Since he was stabbed, he says that he has become a completely different person, and it was a turning point in his life.

Why does Ice think that he was rescued by God that fateful night? "Because I think he knew that I wasn't supposed to be growing up like I did, you know what I'm saying?" he has noted. That is the reason why his music has the positive message it carries in it today.

What was the relationship in time between his introduction to rap music, his racing with Motocross, and his time as a member of the street gangs? Ice has said, "It's all mixed in there. The stabbing was five years ago, in 1986." He's been through a lot of stuff—more than the average person.

Immediately after that he did everything he could to disassociate himself from the street gangs. To this day he does everything he can to distance himself from this era of his life he so strongly regrets being involved in. Does Ice remain in contact with any of his former fellow gang members? "Oh, no. Negative!" is his immediate reply. "The reason why I don't do that is because I'm from the streets." Ice has never forgotten where he came from. While he still loves his friends, he knows that he can't show up in town and have a little private party with all of his former running friends because there could be fighting or other trouble there. Although he used to be into some heavy stuff, he has said that a lot of his friends haven't changed like he did. Ice has completely changed the way he lives, and who he is. He credits God for making him change. He feels he was given a second chance.

"Having gotten stabbed five times really straightened me up. Ever since then, I pray to God every single day. My life is turned around," says Ice. Unfortunately, not all of his old friends have changed. Some are still on what he calls a "gangster trip," with all sorts of fighting and stuff. That's why he wouldn't want to be at a party where there could be any problems.

Since Ice has become successful, he now associates with some of the top people in the record industry. He is very thankful for his position in the music business and the way his career is unfolding. He highly respects Charles Koppelman, the chief executive officer of SBK

Records, and is anxious to disassociate himself from his troubled past.

This is the main reason why, at the beginning of his career, Ice was so emphatic about guarding his true identity. The mystery identity trip was his answer whenever he was questioned about his real name. Since he left the gang, he struggled hard to leave his past behind. The serious trouble with the gangs was involved with Ice's quitting them. When someone wants to quit a gang, it's not so easy to do. You've got to be there to fully understand the reality of it. A member can't just up and leave. According to him, the gang Ice was in was one of the strongest street gangs, and they fought with rival gangs. "There's a lot of stuff that this gang did, and if people find out that I was part of this gang, it stirs up a lot of trouble," he has recalled.

What kind of advice would the Iceman give to his fans who are thinking of joining a gang? "Negative! I'd say, straight from the heart: stay off the streets. It ain't cool. The gang stuff ain't cool, take it from Vanilla Ice." Since he was in it, he knows what he's talking about, and admits it's totally the wrong way to go. He does not support it, and isn't into the whole gangster scene that gangs emulate. According to Ice, the best thing for kids to do is to stay in school, listen to their parents, stay off the drugs, give themselves self-discipline, and think about what they really want to do with their lives.

While still in Miami, Ice was busy with the Motocross circuit and involved with local street gangs, but the sound of rap music was permeating everything he was doing. It was the sound of the ghetto, and all of his friends were heavily into rap. Speaking about some of his primary musical influences, he has recalled, "My inspirations were the Sugarhill Gang, but most of all—James Brown. I was also into Parliament/Funkadelic." He was about thirteen or fourteen at the time. In his mind the first big rap record was the Sugarhill Gang's "Rapper's Delight."

Through his interest in rap music it wasn't long before Vanilla began to try his hand at rapping as well. He was rapping at house parties, on the streets, over at Florida's highway A-1-A, hanging out anywhere and "battling" with other rappers on the scene. He says that initially he was rather quiet while growing up. Then "I started just 'booming.' I was really into it, and dancing too," he says. He also used to break dance at local shopping malls. He would simply pull out a piece of cardboard, and spin on his head. He would pass a little hat and let people throw some money in it. It was great fun for him and it would give him change to go and play video games with.

It was around that same time that he picked up the name "Vanilla." As he explains it, "just because of my complexion, I used to go by Vanilla—I didn't have the Ice on the end of it." Since he grew up in an all-black area, and he was a rapper rapping on the streets, black rappers would see him and say, "Yo, you're vanilla." Ice would be telling them rhymes and stuff off the top of his head, and all of his friends called him and said, "Aw man, that's ice!" "That's smooth!" "That's a cold rap!" From that time to the present, he has always been known as Vanilla, and eventually his moniker was altered to his present handle of Vanilla Ice.

If Ice was going to describe rap music to someone who had never heard it before, how would he define it? "I call it my way of life. It's how I grew up." Ice loves it, and thinks that it's a lot harder than writing any other kind of music, especially as far as singing goes. "When you're singing you can throw in all sorts of 'ooh's' and 'aah's' or 'oooooh girl's,'" says Ice. "When you do rap music, you can't throw stuff like that in." In rap you have to have hundreds of words per song—more than the amount of words you have when you are singing a song. In rap, you have to keep the words flowing— you have to tell a story—and you still have to make the words rhyme. When you're singing it's another art form. Rap is a lot harder than straight singing."

"All I've got to say is, 'Write a rap song, and put it out and see what happens.' Believe me, it won't sell unless you're from the streets and into being a true rapper.

People erroneously think, "Oh, I can make a word rhyme: it's easy." They are surprised to find that it's a lot harder than that, you've got to develop a different style of vocalizing. There is a certain unique style to rapping. Rap music is all about expression—certainly all about street expression. Different rap groups express themselves in a lot of different ways. According to Ice, through the language they use, 2 Live Crew express themselves in the way that they want to express themselves—that's simply them being themselves. Like Ice, they're doing exactly what they want to do. To express himself, Ice doesn't feel he has to curse to rap his message. He still likes and respects Luke and 2 Live Crew and enjoys listening to their music. They're one of his favorite groups, as a matter of fact.

Having just recently recovered from his

near-fatal stabbing and his Motocross accident, Ice was looking forward to possibly finding a new way of expressing himself. While in Dallas, another Motocross competition came up, and he quickly signed up for the races. "That was in 1987 when I was still racing," he recalls. There are a number of good motorcycle tracks in Dallas, Mosher Valley, and Burlison. When he was with Motocross, Ice traveled a good deal.

After the races in Dallas he asked someone what was a good club to go to for some slammin' hip-hop music. Being from the streets, he loves that music, and he was told about a def club called City Lights. So he went to check it out. They played "cold" hip-hop music, and were rockin' the house. With a friend of his, Ice entered the club to check out the scene. The friend announced that he was going to the bathroom, and excused himself. But instead he went to the deejay booth and signed Ice up in a contest. When he came back, he showed Vanilla a piece of paper and said, "Man, I just signed you up in this contest."

Ice is the type of person who, if you dared him to do anything—he'd do it. "Motocross is a real tough sport. I'm from the streets," says Ice, "I'm real tough, so I said, 'Yeah, Okay. I'll get up there and do it.' " He considers himself quite the battle-ax, and since he's a stone-cold rapper at heart, he thought, "Okay, I'll do this for fun. I'll get up there onstage and do this." So, when the time came, he got up onstage. "I did a rhyme, and I did a beatbox—you know: [with that, he demonstrates the a cappella sound of a beatbox like he's "scratching" a record] and then I did a dance off the top of my head. I mean a dance where the deejay had cued the record, and the crowd went nuts, man! They went absolutely nuts. It was great! The deejay at the club that night is out on the road with me now, and his name is Earthquake."

Vanilla Ice had no idea that night that his entire life was about to change. It was through that one totally-by-chance visit to City Lights that he was about to begin several lifelong friendships. The manager of that club was John Bush, who is Ice's road manager now, and the owner of the club was Tommy Quon, who is his career manager now. He signed a contract with Tommy Quon the next day and became one of the fastest artists ever to be signed. "It was like the club that night was what became 'Vanilla Ice on the road' right now! The whole rest of my crew—everybody's from Dallas," says Vanilla.

John Bush proudly recalls that first night he saw this crazy white boy up onstage at the club. "I was one of the first people to discover Vanilla Ice, at the City Lights Club in Dallas," says Bush. "We would have regular talent contests at the club. I'll never forget that first night he got up onstage. He grabbed the mic and busted a rhyme right there. He had Earthquake, the deejay, cue up a record and Ice said to the crowd, 'Now you heard me bust a rhyme/Then you heard me bust a beat/Now check it out, I'm gonna move my feet,' and he began to dance. City Lights is an all-black club, and if you're gonna get up on the stage and dance—especially if you're not black—you had better be good, or people'll start throwing stuff. Well, let me tell you, the crowd was on their feet cheering. I said to Tommy, 'Sign him immediately, this kid's a star!'"

Those few minutes that he spent up onstage that night at City Lights were about to begin a new chapter in his life. He stepped up onstage a streetwise kid without much discipline or direction, but when he stepped off the stage, amid the cheers of the crowd that night, he was on his way to becoming a superstar among rappers.

4

DALLAS ICE

It seems that for Vanilla Ice, that fateful night at the City Lights club in Dallas was really one lucky fluke. A natural-born rapper, he wasn't necessarily seriously competing in the rapping talent contest that night. He was just doing it as a dare. However, that fluke of a performance was to be the beginning of his career as a rap star.

"My friend entered me in the contest," he explained in a newpaper interview, "and I got offstage still thinking it was like a joke, you know like: I wasn't acting like I'm some kind of star or something. I just performed in a talent contest." He had no idea that one day he would have the Number One record in the country. He just walked offstage and sat back down in his seat. The next thing you know, the M.C. announced, "And the winner is Vanilla Ice!" He excitedly jumped up out of his seat. He thought it was great! Then right after the contest, he discovered that Epic, Atlantic, Warner Brothers, Motown, MCA—representatives of all the major record companies—were in the house that night.

Vanilla has recalled, "They approached me right then and there and gave me their business cards, and told me all about themselves." The very next day he signed the contracts with his new manager, Tommy Quon.

That night, club manager John Bush had taken Ice's phone number, and the next day Ice was invited back to the club to meet with Tommy. At that time, Quon had managed several other rap artists, but had yet to have really crossed any one of them over to mass popularity. Among the acts he was managing were The Mac Band, Mikki Bleu, Out of the Blue, Don Diego and Greg Smith. Don Diego and Benita Arterberry were signed to Tommy's own record label, Ultrax Records; Mikki Bleu was on EMI Records; and The Mac Band was on MCA.

Ice has recalled that at his first meeting,

Tommy told him that he needed a manager. Ice didn't really know much about what he was doing, but luckily he was in the right hands. He credits God for playing a good role in that part of his life as well.

Right on the spot, Ice instinctively got a good vibe from Tommy and genuinely felt that he could trust Quon's judgment, and he signed a management contract right there. It wasn't long after that, that Vanilla decided to make Dallas his permanent home base. "When I was younger," he has explained, "I had moved around a lot. I lived a whole bunch of different places. I lived in Dallas, I lived in some parts of California, and I lived in Miami." He had moved from place to place but then he decided to move back to Dallas, right after he signed with Tommy. Dallas was where everything started happening for him, and his stepfather was there to look out for him.

As Ice began to put his performing act together, under the guidance of Tommy Quon, he was utilizing all local talent from the Dallas area, so it made sense for him to have that city as his home as well. That's where all of the crew was from, and he wanted to be around them, because that's where the whole thing started: "Vanilla Ice" was born right there on the spot. He was still racing Motocross at the time, and he raced for about another year after that. But everything was just going downhill because of the ankles. Everything just seemed messed up. So he got out of racing.

Besides making sense from a business standpoint, for Vanilla being a professional rapper was a way out of the whole street gang scene. As Ice has said, "It was more like the start of a dream coming true, and that's exactly what happened to me—a dream came true."

Ice had already amassed a catalogue of several rap songs he had written. Starting with those first songs, Ice and Tommy began to develop his act. He'd always been writing rap songs, Vanilla explains, "not for anything special, just for use on the streets, you know, just to 'battle' people and stuff." He did it just for fun." He wrote his own rhymes all the time, and became proficient at it.

Then Vanilla signed up with Tommy, making Tommy Ice's personal manager. Tommy began to get a record deal together. Both Vanilla and Tommy started to get Ice's career under way. Tommy explained to Vanilla what kind of a career was possible if carefully planned, and together they began to pursue their vision.

"Tommy Quon is an amazing guy," says Peter Seitz, who is Vanilla's booking agent. "He had such a vision when he saw Vanilla, and he changed him into the star he is today."

As he stated, Ice assumed from Tommy Quon's exquisite clothes and sharp appearance that he was rolling in money. Although he had operating capital to keep the two clubs Tommy owned running (he owned Monopoly as well as City Lights), he too was banking on one day hitting the big time with one of his clients. The next years they worked hard, and then the SBK Records deal came along in 1990.

They survived by playing various club dates—Tommy knew a lot of club owners as a result of owning two clubs of his own. Ice was kept busy working at several local clubs, creating a strong act and developing his own flashy stage presence. It helped him a lot. Now many people think that he's coming right out of the box, because the "To the Extreme" album has become a multi-million-seller over the past few months. Outside of Dallas, people had not generally heard of Vanilla Ice until "Ice Ice Baby" broke on the charts. From performing in those clubs in Texas, he became known all over the Dallas area, and it helped him to put his act together. When he first appeared nationally, everyone was saying things like: "Wow—he can really get down!"

"Good stage presence!" as though he had just begun doing it. Of course, this was not his first time onstage.

Vanilla Ice started out working in the clubs. Then he began opening for other acts. From there he started getting booked on shows, like the "Stop the Violence" tour with Ice-T, Public Enemy, Stetsasonic, Sir Mix-A-Lot. He did several shows with them in Oklahoma City and Dallas. He also did a couple of M. C. Hammer tour dates, opening up for him in Tyler, Texas, a couple of times. He also opened for Rodney O. and Joe Cooley, Cash Money, 2 Live Crew, Easy E, and The Doc.

Along the way, Vanilla had several great experiences, in which he was able to meet and open shows for many of his favorite performers. He opened for Paula Abdul at Monopoly in Dallas about a year and a half ago, when she was just starting out. He was thrilled when she pulled him out onstage during her performance. He was on the side of the stage watching her, and at the end of her performance while they were dancing, she pulled him onstage so that he could dance with her. He appreciates this. She also went to his concert in San Diego and introduced him on the stage. Since that first night at Monopoly, Ice has remained friends with Paula, and she is one of his favorite people in the business.

Recently, he was the opening act for one of his favorite groups, 2 Live Crew. For him it was a dream come true. "That was great, man. They got off, and they were slamming at City Lights. It was great. It was super dope!" Vanilla Ice has said.

He also opened for Tone Loc in Oklahoma City. For a while it looked like Tone Loc was going to be the first rapper to hit the Number One spot on the pop singles charts with his hits "Wild Thing" and "Funky Cold Medina," but he stopped short at Number Two. He was subsequently unable to come up with a follow-up single to those cuts. Tone Loc lost his writer, Young MC, who branched off into his own career. Young MC had written "Wild Thing" and "Funky Cold Medina." Predicts Ice, "I don't think Tone is gonna have a hit as big as those two songs ever. He might have another hit, but it won't be as big as either one of those songs." This is not a dilemma that Ice is going to have to face in his own career since he is capable of writing his own material.

That immediately brings up the question of: "How much of Vanilla Ice's image and 'look' is his own, and how much was created under the direction of Tommy Quon?" "Actually, it's just me," Ice has explained. "That's me, and that's the way I've been for a long time—it's just me." He didn't have anything planned as far as image goes for the album. He looked that way before he even imagined that he was going to have an album out! He dressed that way—those are all his own clothes. It's just him: Ice, Ice, Ice.

And how about the haircut? He has said that he had the lines cut into his hair since he was in the eighth grade. The white streaks were put in the front of his hair about three years ago, and the cuts in his eyebrows were put in about a year and a half ago.

Okay, now it's time for the really major question: How does he get his hair to stand up on end like that? It looks like he would have to hang upside down on a bar to get it to stand up like that! Ice has explained that he uses a product called Vital Care Super Spritz. "It's real good. It's like super glue. There's nothing that can touch it. It's real stiff, man!" It certainly gives Ice a distinctive look.

All right, the image was in place, the clothes were fly, the sound was supersonic, and the hair was straight up in the air. Now, the only thing that was missing was the hit record. That was next on the agenda.

During this same time period, Ice and Quon

began going into the studio and recording his rap songs. Their next objective was to land a record deal. That, however, was not as easy a task as they had hoped. Tommy shopped the album to all of the major labels, but to sign Ice, the record companies didn't want to pay them the amount of money they wanted. Ice and Tommy were concerned that he would be "lost like a needle in a haystack. So we held out. Tommy's a great manager." If it were up to Ice, he would have taken the very first deal he was offered, but fortunately Tommy's a good manager, and he wouldn't accept a deal that wasn't up to his standards. He was holding out for the right recording deal, and Vanilla would get mad at him sometimes, and complain that he was ready to sign a contract and was tired of waiting. But Tommy kept insisting that they didn't want a bad deal. They ended up holding out for a couple of years, for the right deal. Finally, with SBK, the right deal came through.

However, before that Tommy decided to create his own record label, which he called Ultrax Records. He hired a distributor in Atlanta. Ultrax Records is Tommy's label and was originally distributed through Ichiban Records, in Atlanta. (Ichiban means "Number One" in Japanese.) Curtis Mayfield is signed to Ichiban.

Forty-eight thousand copies of Ice's album, called "Hooked," were sold in two or three weeks. It was different from the "To the Extreme" album, although "To the Extreme" has remixes of some of the songs off of "Hooked." However, they were totally remixed and don't even sound like the same songs.

The success of the "Hooked" album was based on the overwhelming popularity of Vanilla Ice's first single. It was a two-sided single, with "Play That Funky Music" as the A side, and "Ice Ice Baby" as the B side. For some reason, "Play That Funky Music" wasn't doing anything on the charts, until one particular deejay made a fortunate mistake and played the wrong side of the single on the radio. The man was Darrell J., the morning deejay on radio station WAGH-FM in Columbus, Georgia. As Darrell J. recalls, "I saw this white guy with a pretty lady on an album cover. I put it on and everyone started smiling. I said, 'Play it. This is a hit!'" Sure enough—he was one hundred percent correct.

In fact, the album started to take off so quickly that Tommy Quon's Ultrax Records couldn't keep up with the demand for copies of it. That's where SBK Records came into the picture. Here Tommy and Ice had this record that was Number One in Dallas, Texas; Number One in Columbus, Georgia; and Number One in Chattanooga, Tennessee. The small record company couldn't manufacture it fast enough. Then all of a sudden—SBK came through. Actually they were close to signing with Atlantic Records.

SBK Records was already on a hot streak in 1990, having had phenomenal success with the Wilson Phillips album and their two huge Number One hits: "Hold On" and "Release Me." Songs were quickly remixed and mastered, and all of a sudden the new version of "Ice Ice Baby," and the new album "To the Extreme" were released. The next thing you know—Vanilla Ice was on the launching pad and prepared to take off into the great unknown. With the album and single released onto the marketplace, the only thing that was needed was exposure. That's where the phenomenally successful M. C. Hammer tour came into place. Fasten your seat belt, Ice, you're ready for blast-off!

THE SOUND OF ICE

In the world of pop music—whether that encompasses rock, rap, dance, r&b, or country—the bottom line is what the music sounds like. If there is a strong song and the timing is right and the record makes it into the Top Ten, a hit can make it on the merit of the song and the performance alone. An equally important factor is the singer—or the rapper—and what his popularity is at any given moment.

Take for example Lisa Stansfield and her phenomenal 1990 Number One hit "All Around the World." When that song was released, no one had ever heard of Lisa Stansfield, so her image and her name had nothing to do with the success of the record. However, when Madonna released "Vogue" a couple of months later and it too became a huge Number One hit, was it a hit because the song was so strong, or because it was by Madonna?

In the case of Vanilla Ice's first SBK single, "Ice Ice Baby," which was destined for the Number One slot, most people didn't know Vanilla Ice. Like Lisa Stansfield, the success of "Ice Ice Baby" was due, for the most part, to the appeal of the song itself. Now the question arises: Was the runaway success of Ice's second single, "Play That Funky Music," due to the success of "Ice Ice Baby" or was it due to the strength of the song itself? The fact of the matter is that: (1) everyone knew who Ice was, and it was in part his image and his track record that made people anticipate his next release, and (2) "Play That Funky Music" is a fantastic song.

Since Ice's album "To the Extreme" also made it all the way to the top and sold millions of copies in a matter of weeks, it is obviously due to the fact that the public doesn't just care about one of his songs—they love all of the songs on the album. Yes, Ice's def image is fresh and exciting, but the bottom line is the fact that his music is great.

Let's look at his songs from the "To the Extreme" album.

Just by looking at his lyrics, you'll learn about the Iceman, since he puts all of his life experiences into his music. In "Ice Ice Baby," Ice wrote about growing up in the streets and the things that go on there. A lot of people out there are trying to make him look like he's trying to be something other than what he is. They're saying that he's not really from the streets.

He has indicated that the press has not given him credit for having lived the kind of life that he actually led, and that it continually questions him on this subject. Critics say that M. C. Hammer and Ice's raps are "soft" or don't have an authentic edge. "Like it's not as true as a real street rapper," he says. He attributes this to the fact that he's selling a lot of records, and that the jealous and critical rappers are not.

The song "Stop That Train," which Ice co-wrote with M. C. Smooth, is a fictional story about a girl who is into sex games. But like all of Ice's music, it's not obscene at all, in fact, it's clean compared to other people's rap. It's obviously sexually explicit and about a girl who is into bizarre sex games. The song portrays the Iceman commanding, "Stop this train, baby!" because he wants to get off. In other words, the train is her fantasy, that has turned into his nightmare.

"Hooked" is a song about a guy who is madly in love with a girl. In fact, Ice has a dialogue with one of the posse members in the middle of the rap. In this way he is offering advice to someone who is hooked on a girl. It features an expressive sax solo that makes this one of the most memorable cuts on the album.

"Ice Is Workin' It" is a song written out of his natural stream of consciousness, and is clearly addressed to jealous rappers who thought that Ice would never make it to number one. He is heard bragging about his accomplishments.

And "Play That Funky Music" is about the same in terms of structure and approach. Ice basically let the lyrics flow. By listening to it you'll find the lyrics to be more streetish and harsh. Inspired by the 1970s hit of the same name by the group Wild Cherry, Ice's new reworking of that theme is an across-the-board hit and a fabulous rap that is getting international airplay.

A special "radio mix" was done by Gail Scott King, who is highly respected in the music industry. The song almost immediately jumped to the top ten on several radio stations' playlists. On one station it made a jump from number forty to number four in one week's time! Right about then it was crystal clear that Ice had another hit on his hands.

"Life Is a Fantasy" is a song about a dream, which everyone can understand. It is reminiscent of the Eric Burdon and War song "Spill the Wine." Like Burdon, Ice fantasizes and daydreams about a girl and a passionate encounter. The main difference is that Ice has just one girl, and Burdon had the attention of several girls in his song. The pace of the song isn't typical of rap artists, and this is what makes the whole album interesting—Ice has more than one gear to his raps. The jammin' cut features a provocative drum roll that gives the song its infectious feeling. The bass line is very much a "Miami"-inspired beat.

The song "Dancin'" is, as the title says, about dancing. It's just a hyped cut, expressly meant to rock the crowd, to pump them up with high energy, to get his fans involved in the music.

"Go Ill" has more of a New York beat. It uses a live drummer rather than drum machines. The drum, bass guitar, electric guitar, string bass, and keyboards create more of a New York sound. It doesn't have a lot of bass. As Ice knows, New York has its own kind of style, and there's not as much bass as in the classic Miami sound.

"It's a Party" is a song that is about two rappers "battling" at a house party. Since all rappers brag nonstop about themselves, the song carries the whole party atmosphere, complete with the chorus sounding as though the other partygoers are cheering the rappers on.

Ice gave "To the Extreme" a little bit of versatility, so that its appeal is not only to rap fans. That's why the song "Rosta Man" is on the album. Not everybody loves that song immediately, but a lot of people do pick it as their favorite song on the album, especially Ice's older audience, such as the parents of his fans. The same is true for the ballad, "I Love You." It appeals to people on a different level.

The song "Rosta Man" brings to mind the question of other artists who influenced Ice. He listens avidly to the music of UB40, Nami, and Bob Marley. Not only has Ice claimed in the press that he likes Bob Marley's music, but he is a huge fan of reggae, period.

The song "I Love You" is a ballad, done by his co-writer Kim Sharp, who also produced it. It features a saxophone solo by Don Diego, who really jams on it. Since that song is about love, many people say that his rap is too light, but a lot of hard-core rap fans really gravitate

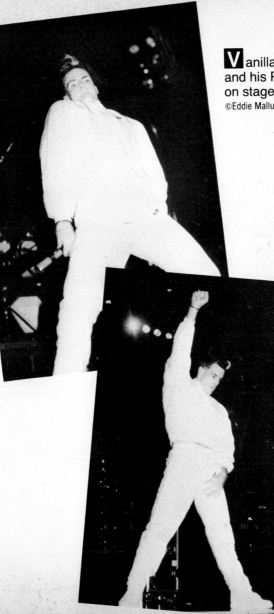

Vanilla Ice
and his Posse
on stage.
©Eddie Malluk/Retna Ltd.

Vanilla Ice electrifying the audience with his rapping and dancing.

©Eddie Malluk/Retna Ltd.

Ice maxin' and relaxin'.
©Todd Kaplan, Star File Photos

Ice is almost as well known for his cold good looks as for his music.

Vanilla Ice singing "I Love You" in performance.
©Larry Busacca/Retna Ltd.

Vanilla Ice "To the Extreme"
©Kahn/Retna Ltd.

Backstage with Ice
©Todd Kaplan/Star File Photos

That boy can dance!
©Eddie Malluk/Retna Ltd.

Vanilla Ice up close. Ice has had the lines cut into his hair since he was in the eighth grade.

©Todd Kaplan/Star File Photos

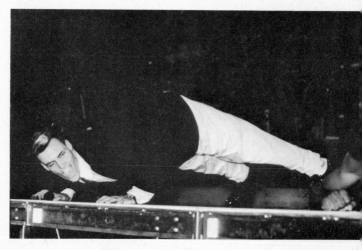

Ice busts into a dance.
©Todd Kaplan/Star File Photos

Ice gets down.
©Michael Lavine/Outline Press

©Eddie Malluk/Retna Ltd.

Ice's smooth style sells out concerts from Tallahassee to Tacoma.

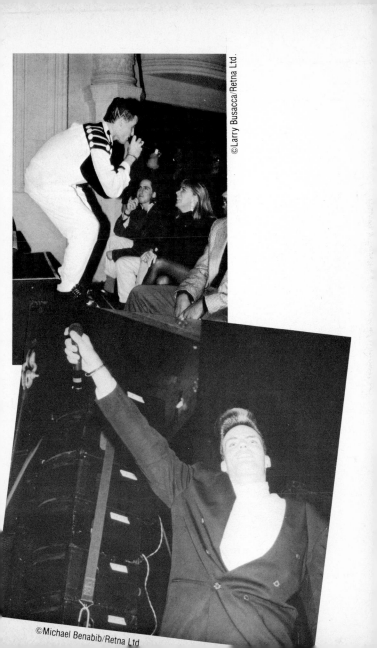

With his incredible good luck and drive, Ice has his sights set on becoming a movie star.

The future of rap music: Ice, Ice, Ice.
©Michael Lavine/Outline Press

toward that song. Yes, he's a full hard-core rapper at heart, but Ice clearly wants to be versatile, so he can appeal to more than just the hard-core rap listeners. That's the logical explanation of why he made his album as varied as he did.

"Having a Roni," which is a short rhyme at the end of the album, is about a young "fly girl." Ice does the song complete with a "beat box." According to Ice, a "fly girl" is someone who is fancy and has her nails done regularly; her makeup is always flawless.

The "To the Extreme" album was the first production ever to be recorded at the Loomis Studio. Paul Loomis, who is its owner, is also a great engineer. In addition, George Anderson played on several of the tracks. Anderson is a master musician who plays just about every instrument there is: keyboards and six-string bass on "Ice Is Workin' It." He also plays keyboards on "Play That Funky Music."

Ice has claimed that the 2 Live Crew censorship controversy and case has not affected his act, or his lyrics, at all. "Rap music is about expression," says Ice, "and 2 Live Crew is expressing themselves the way that they want to, and they're selling a lot of albums that way." While some people claim that their act is obscene and highly objectionable, Vanilla Ice still ranks them as one of his favorite groups of all time. He doesn't care for their message, but he still loves their music.

Neither has the case caused people to criticize Ice's act. He says that he doesn't have to worry about censorship, because he doesn't curse to express himself. "The censorship law really has nothing to do with me," Ice has said, "but if I wanted to curse, I would." 2 Live Crew doesn't get as much airplay as Vanilla Ice, although they're selling albums and doing what they want to do. Basically that's what Ice is doing as well—doing what he wants to do, and expressing himself his way—aboveground. In other words, Ice didn't have to change any of the lyrics on his album because they were clean to begin with.

"Ice Ice Baby" has brought Ice phenomenal success. It was one that really went over the top, out of all of the rap songs that have come before. Ice attributes this success to the fact that it's a completely different style of rap music. When it hit the charts, it didn't sound like any other song that's out there; it was simply something new for people to step to.

One controversy that surrounds "Ice Ice Baby" is the copyright problem of sampling the bass line from "Under Pressure" by David Bowie and Queen. It was sampled right off of that record about two and a half years ago. Then when "Ice Ice Baby" became a Number One hit, problems developed. David Bowie and Queen (Freddie Mercury, Brian May, John Deacon, and Roger Taylor) wanted credit for their part. They were credited in *Billboard* and on the subsequent labels, and they now receive songwriting credit for their bass lines. The matter of copyright infringement is still being worked out with attorneys for both sides.

For readers of this book who don't understand what "sampling" is, it is simply recording a series of notes with a drum machine or synthesizer. It allows a musician to play back the sound, or cut the treble end off of it, or the bass end off of it, or totally truncate it. You can push a button and have the "sampled" chord sound come in like a beat in a drum machine, or you can hit another button to get a snare drum or cymbals, or you can hit still another button to play all three separate sounds. You can then put it all back together in song form, add a number of other instruments that you have chosen, and end up with your own unique sound.

This new way of making music has opened the door up for all sorts of yet-to-be-solved copyright problems. Does the new mutated version of the chord belong to the original musician, or to the recording engineer who creates the "sample" of it? Therein the controversy lies.

In another copyright arrangement, the writers of the original Wild Cherry song "Play That Funky Music" are now receiving co-writing credit for Ice's song of the same name.

Vanilla Ice is excited about his videos as well. The "Play That Funky Music" video is comprised of live concert shots that were filmed in Toronto and Montreal, Canada. A crew came to his show on the Hammer tour, and filmed, and came up with a video. Ice's third video is for "Stop That Train," which will be his third single. "The 'Stop That Train' video is like a movie," Ice has said. Ice stresses that the video is the result of the producer's talent and hard work, and he was genuinely thrilled with the production of this visually exciting video. He hopes that one day it will win an MTV Award.

As Ice recounted on an MTV interview, he had a lot of fun filming the video for "Stop That Train." He had to lie down on a stretch of railroad tracks, where he was tied down, surrounded by several young "hotties," as he refers to sexy girls. A train started to come while he was tied down to the tracks. "I jumped up and ran like mad! Everyone was running around shouting, 'Get him up quick!' It scared me at first!" he exclaims.

The video package entitled "Vanilla Ice— Play That Funky Music, White Boy" contains three videos, including some home videos, some backstage shots, some rehearsal shots, and behind the scenes shots. It was released in late November. The platinum-selling Ice-Man's stocking stuffer for Christmas included the three heart-melting rap 'n' roll videos: "Play That Funky Music," "Stop That Train," and the number one single "Ice Ice Baby."

ICE IS WORKIN' IT

The phenomenal success of Vanilla was a brilliant combination of talent, exposure, and timing. These three elements all worked in his favor. Talent: Ice was polished, poised, and ready to really kick it. Exposure: he connected with the M. C. Hammer tour just as his album was released, and promoted it to the max. And timing: Middle America was simply ready to accept rap music.

His debut SBK album, "To the Extreme," and his single "Ice Ice Baby" both hit the charts in September. By November he was the hottest new star in the country, with over four million albums, and one million singles sold.

The next thing you know: Vanilla Ice is negotiating movie deals!

According to Ken Lane, the senior director of Top 40 Radio at SBK Records, "It's a combination of phenomenal airplay, phenomenal press, and a vibe among radio, that when the record is played, it reacts instantaneously with all demographics and it sells on first listen. It's a 'one listen record.' He's the first rapper to have a Number One record in *Billboard*. Neither M. C. Hammer nor Tone Loc nor Young MC's 'Bust a Move' went to Number One in *Billboard* on the "Hot 100" chart. They all peaked at Number Two or Three. America was ready for a white rapper who raps positive. There's no negativity in his raps. He is totally antigang and antidrug, and that is also his personal values. He practices what he preaches. He's never touched drugs; he's a total athlete. He works out and he performs in a very athletic way. He is someone who is on a natural high, as opposed to a chemical high. You know that when he's out there on stage, he's enjoying it for the sake of enjoying it. He's not spacey or anything. He just has a total vibe and a total dedication to his profession."

On the subject of Ice's future, Lane says, "I think that his audience base is now built, and it's going to expand from the three million people who have already bought the album. It is triple platinum-plus, and this thing keeps building and building. There is no end in sight, and he is going to begin playing his own tour, playing between twenty-five hundred- and five thousand-seat arenas and then he'll go out and do big big Madison Square Garden types of venues. His tour runs from January sixteenth to February twenty-fourth, then a break, then arenas . . . now being set up."

With regard to SBK Records' role in Ice's career, Lane explains, "The company's been behind him from day one, and there's been a belief in Vanilla Ice, and it stems all of the way from the top. And, without that belief, when you go to radio to promote the music, it's never gonna happen. They've got to believe in you, you have to believe in the record, and then the record has got to perform. And with this record, all three facets happened beautifully, combined with a strong press presence."

Peter Seitz, who is Vanilla Ice's booking agent, has watched the plotting of Ice's career since the early days when he was just starting out in clubs as an opening act. "I got involved on his first label, which was in Atlanta," he explains, "and I was instrumental in putting him on the M. C. Hammer tour. By incessantly telling everyone involved how good he was going to be, they finally took a listen, and agreed that he was perfect for the tour. I've been with Tommy since the beginning." Seitz notes that Ice moved from his original agency to Famous Artists Agency headed by Jerry Ade. As Seitz explains: "That's the same agency that made New Kids on the Block. Jerry is an amazing agent. He's the one who brought New Kids on the Block to Tiffany when she needed an opening act. They performed a cappella in an office for Tiffany and she liked them. That's how they broke. Jerry's got great insight. When Vanilla Ice came over, they brought me over from I.C.M. [International Creative Management].

"From the word go, people who didn't even know the music went crazy when they saw him on tour with M. C. Hammer," Seitz continues. "He dances more than M. C. Hammer on stage! He joined the M. C. Hammer tour on September 19, 1990, in Cedar Rapids, Iowa, and his record just came out a couple of weeks before. Very rarely does something like that happen. M. C. Hammer sold six million albums and was on the charts for twenty-two weeks. I told Tommy Quon, the manager, after the Vanilla Ice album had been out two weeks, that Ice was going to bump Hammer out of the Number One spot. M. C. Hammer continued to stay Number One for about eight more weeks, but then he bumped him. Here he is out on tour with M. C. Hammer with only one single out, and he bumps him out of the Number One slot on the Pop Albums chart, after eight weeks. I believed that Vanilla's album was destined for Number One and I told Tommy Quon what was going to happen. I always knew this guy was going to be big."

Citing the reason for Ice's success in the music business, Seitz claims that, "Tommy and Vanilla Ice are the two most 'straight up' people I've ever dealt with. They're really just great people. They're very thankful for everything that's ever been given to them. They've got no ego trips."

When Ice signed with SBK Records, he and Tommy had almost signed a contract with Atlantic Records. Suddenly the SBK deal materialized, and topped Atlantic's offer. It was the chief executive officer of SBK who was insistent that he sign with his label. As Ice refers to him: "Charles Koppelman, the head boss, the head honcho.

"He wanted me. We had our cards on the table, Atlantic had a pretty good deal there. Then Charles Koppelman came through and threw his cards on the table, and it beat Atlantic's deal," stated Ice. He and Tommy decided to go with SBK, which turned out to be a great move. They are both thrilled with how accommodating and helpful everyone at the label has been.

Koppelman says of Ice, "His raps are wholesome and positive, nothing that's going to upset anybody . . . He's a handsome kid, a good dancer—the kind of artist that would attract a strong female following."

"The nice thing about Ice," says his road manager, John Bush, "is the fact that he has never forgotten any of the people from when he was starting out. He's like family, and I think of him as my son. All of us on the road are real tight."

Things are about to heat up even further now that projects are underway to turn Vanilla Ice into a movie star. He's already filmed his part in the forthcoming movie, *Teenage Mutant Ninja Turtles II: The Secret of the Ooze*. How did that come about? "Actually they called us," Ice explains. "They wanted us. The way it happened is a real trip, because I talked to the executive producer—I guess that's what he was—one of the head honchos, and they gave us all director's chairs with our names on them. They said, 'Teenage Mutant Ninja Turtles II/Vanilla Ice.' All of my dancers got them with their names on them as well. This head honcho guy's son is madly crazed over Vanilla Ice. He said, 'Yo, Dad, you ought to get him in the movie!' So he did! He called us and wanted us."

According to Ice, "I play myself in the film. They had a whole stage built for me that said 'Vanilla Ice' on it, all custom made. It was real cool, and I got a lot of close-ups. The Teenage Mutant Ninja Turtles held me up one time and did a lot of choreographing. We danced with the Turtles and were choreographed in the movie with the Turtles; it was really cool." The scene that transpires is the first scene he is in. He is up onstage, doing a show and performing while the Turtles are talking backstage with the promoters. All of a sudden the Turtles burst onto the stage like they're having a fight. This all comes as Ice is ending the song, and going off of the rap. The producers captured the whole rap song on film, which is the theme song for the movie, and it's called "Ninja Rap."

In addition to the American version of the film, Ice also had to record a special rendition of the song for the Japanese market. "We had to change the word 'Ninja' for over there [Japan] because Ninja is sacred." They changed the word to 'hero' so that in Japan the title is *Teenage Mutant Hero Turtles*."

Not only is the song slated for inclusion on the film's soundtrack album, but it is also due to be released as a single as well. The film itself is going to open on March 22, 1991, and, claims Ice, "It's great! There's some great fight scenes, and they have some new characters in the movie. There's this one huge seven-foot-tall guy dressed as a monster creature, and he's fighting with the Turtles while I'm on the stage, and the promoters are backstage going, 'What's going on?'" In the scene, Ice basically performed his song amid the action. As far as having a role, Ice didn't have a lot of dialogue, but he did get a great deal of screen time. It's a pretty large scene, and you'll be able to see a lot of him in the movie.

While he was filming *Teenage Mutant Ninja Turtles II*, Ice celebrated his twenty-second birthday. According to him, "It was the best birthday I've ever had, no doubt about it— definitely, by far!" He was in Wilmington, North Carolina, on the set of the movie. He claims that he was totally surprised. He was awarded his plaques for his double platinum album, his platinum single, and his platinum cassette. He was also presented with his *Billboard* Number One certification.

His mother and his brother were there. They started from the hotel, all piled into a limousine, and Ice didn't have any idea where they were heading. Then, all of a sudden he saw where they were going: to the set of the movie. Vanilla suspected that they were up to something, but he didn't think it was going to be "extreme" or anything like it was. He was ecstatically surprised at the lavish party they threw for him.

That film had barely been shot when negotiations began for Ice's next film role. Tommy and Ice had been sent the script for the last chapter of *Nightmare on Elm Street*. Ice has explained, "They wanted me to play this guy named Jason, which is really acting. I was talking to them and telling them, 'I really don't know how to act.'" The character of Jason is an orphan from a foster home. His parents were killed a long time ago by Freddie Kruger. At the foster home, he's considered a ladies' man, kind of like a James Dean type. He drives a motorcycle. He's kind of rough, but kind of like Ice. The script that Ice was sent was approximately three hundred pages long. Unfortunately, Tommy and Ice ultimately decided that the role wasn't the right career move at this time.

Only months ago Vanilla Ice was a regional performer who was basically unknown to the American public. However, in a mere matter of weeks he has been transformed into an international sensation. Ice has had a whirlwind courtship with fame. He was in Europe at the end of December. Everything heated up in Europe when "Ice Ice Baby" hit Number One in England and Number Three in Germany. He was supposed to go for three months, but he was forced to cut down on the European tour because of his much-demanded tour schedule in the United States. SBK kept him busy while the single was in demand—while it became very hot. It was part of their Vanilla Ice marketing strategy.

In addition to everything else that has been happening in the Ice camp, there are also several endorsement deals under way. Several companies want to be associated with the Iceman.

Nothing has been signed yet, but among the companies that have been mentioned previously in the press are Nike, Coke, and British Knights. Big things are happening right and left for Vanilla Ice. If he plays his cards right, he just might wind up as the James Dean of the 1990s!

THE ICE CONTROVERSY

It was the third week in November of 1990 that I began putting the Vanilla Ice story on paper. At the time, Ice was also doing a photo shoot for the cover of *Rolling Stone* magazine and an extensive interview for a story in *People*. His true identity had not yet surfaced in the press by then.

On Friday, November 16, a press story broke about the recording duo Milli Vanilli and the scandalous fact that neither of the group's members, Rob Pilatus and Fab Morvan, had anything to do with their multi-platinum album. In fact, neither of the guys sang on any of their recordings or live appearances. At that point, I had this sneaking suspicion that Ice's "cover" could be blown at any point. Sure enough, on Monday, November 19, *USA Today* ran an item which in part read: "On the heels of the Milli Vanilli scandal comes a report that Vanilla Ice is not the ghetto-bred motorcyle champion he claims to be. *The Dallas Morning News* says the white rapper is Robert Van Winkle, who attended high school in an affluent Dallas suburb and did not win three national Motocross championships, as claimed. Previously, *The Miami Herald* debunked Ice's claim that he once attended the same Miami high school as 2 Live Crew's Luther Campbell. Ice and his publicists have issued a revised bio."

Ice and his representatives have confirmed that Ice had indeed been born Robert Van Winkle, and that his nickname was Robby. With regard to the Motocross championships, they were "regional" competitions that Ice participated in, and never did he specifically say that he had won "national" competitions, as some papers had reported. Ice did attend high school in Miami, but at North Miami Beach High School. What he had failed to mention to the press was the fact that he had moved to Dallas during high school and *also* attended a high school there.

In addition to the explosion of publicity that

Ice was getting for his mystery identity and the facts that were awry, there was also trouble in the M. C. Hammer/Vanilla Ice camps, backstage at the concerts. M. C. Hammer's brother and manager took Ice aside and confronted him with "dissin'" Hammer offstage to the press. In the middle of all of this controversy, as the mystery of Ice's true identity was slowly unraveling, he was interviewed by *People* magazine. The article, which was published on December 3, 1990, exposed his real name and many other details about his life that Ice did not want to let out. Ice had finally told *People* magazine the truth because he felt obligated to set the record straight.

Some of the facts that *People* magazine had dug up, Ice had wanted to forget about. He admitted publicly to giving away "a couple of false facts, so I could mislead people, so they couldn't look me up and find out where I live." Ice has said he also wanted to protect his mother and his privacy. He confessed, "I used to be into some bad stuff." As Ice recently explained in the press, "I'm supposed to be a role model for kids now. I didn't want people to find out who I really was." He was also worried about someone finding and bothering his mother. Now Ice would have to move his mother. Fortunately Ice had already picked out a new house for her.

Ice admitted that he had faced "racism and stuff." Some people, he explained, don't give him credit as a rapper because he is white. One reporter in Macon, Georgia, told him "Ice Ice Baby" was the only good song on the album. But since the album had sold four million as of the previous day, Ice obviously had nothing to worry about.

Ice stated unequivocally that he had never attended Palmetto High School in Miami and claimed that he had never said he had. He said he had nothing to do with the phrase "The Elvis of Rap," which also appeared in the press bio. That phrase, he explained, was coined by the record company.

M. C. Hammer had also entered the controversy. Ice had been quoted in a Macon paper saying that M. C. Hammer's T-shirts and souvenirs were not selling as well as his. Ice adamantly denied saying anything like this. According to Ice, Louis Burrell, M. C. Hammer's brother and manager, had shown Ice a copy of the article after a show one night. Ice has said that he told him, "Man, I don't know what's going on. I never said that."

Ice has only good things to say about M. C. Hammer. He was grateful to Hammer for giving him the opportunity to come on the tour. He also said he thought it was helping him to sell albums. Ice claimed that he had known M. C. Hammer since before Hammer's first album came out. "He's a homie of mine," Ice insisted. "We're good friends."

Ice and Hammer are often compared, since they were on the same tour and occupied the top spots on the pop charts. Ice regrets the comparisons. He claimed that he and Hammer were in no way competing with each other. "We're not anything alike, and I love Hammer to death," Ice said. He has adamantly insisted that he was not "dissin'" Hammer. "Never have, never will." However, Ice recognizes that there is inevitably a "friendly competition" among all singing and rapping groups vying for spots on the pop charts. "They all are, after all, fighting for the Number One spot on the charts."

Ice has also spoken about the phenomenal success of his T-shirts, one of which he designed himself. Forty-four thousand dollars worth had been sold in just one night! The front of one of the T-shirts features a brick wall background with arrows in it and a street painting airbrushed on it. "Vanilla" is written out in a jagged style of type, and "Ice is made out of ice cubes." On the back, it reads "Vanilla

Ice, To the Extreme Tour 1990." It's black with fluorescent colors on it. Another T-shirt has a picture of Ice on the front in turquoise and orange—the Miami Dolphins' colors. On the back "Vanilla Ice" is featured on a patch.

Ice's stabbing, which left the large scar on his leg, was also discussed in the *People* magazine article. Ice explained that although he was actually stabbed in Richardson, Texas, he had originally said that he was stabbed in Coconut Grove, Florida. He did this, he explained, "so old gang members couldn't look me up. People still don't like me." He also explained that he only "misled" various people to protect his family and preserve their privacy.

Ice's stabbing caused him to reassess his life. "I was close to dying—real close," Ice said. To make matters worse, Ice has type A-B Negative blood, which is very hard to come by. Time was running out quickly and the hospital could not find a blood donor. Luckily, a donor came through at the last minute.

Ice's stay at Medical City Hospital wasn't all bad, even though it lasted over New Year's. Ice has told about a party the staff let him throw in his room. "They allowed everybody to come up past midnight, and everything," he said, laughingly recalling it.

Ice also explained that the other facts in the *People* article are accurate. The guy who stabbed him, Ice has confirmed, was from a rival gang. Ice has various scars to prove the stabbing occurred. At the time of the stabbing, as Ice has repeatedly noted, "I was actually taking up for [defending] a friend of mine when that happened."

Ice has also talked about having moved around a lot. "We lived in a lot of places in Miami and Dallas when I was growing up," he said recently. "We didn't have money." Perhaps this moving about accounts for some of the confusion with the high schools he attended. His stepfather at that time, Byron Miño, lived in Dallas. Ice is grateful to Miño, even though he and Ice's mother are no longer married. Ice has said Miño has helped him out a great deal and looked after him. "He's been there for me," Ice said. "Byron as well as my mother are the people who have helped me out the most."

VANILLA'S DEF DICTIONARY

Yo, homeboys and homegirls, listen up: "If you're makin' the scene and poppin' and chillin', and somebody dis's you and you feel like you're illin', get your battle rhyme together so it's soundin' real nice, and before you know it you'll be livin' large and maxin' like a cube of ice."

If you can read the above rap, and emerge from it without a bewildered look on your face, chances are you won't need this chapter for profilin' with the other rappers in your neighborhood. However, if you need to brush up on your rap lingo—here it is—the deffest dictionary of street talk ever compiled. Without further ado—just so your rap is better, here's a def dictionary—as if Ice were Webster:

Aboveground
It means not going "underground"—going where the radio will play it is the meaning of *aboveground*. There are several groups who don't care if they're on the radio or not, because they use "blue" language on every song on the album, that's "underground." Ice's songs are totally "aboveground."

Battle
Like war. A battle in MC language or rappers language, means: two rappers around a crowd, without any music. Maybe someone would do a beatbox, and one rapper would start dissin' the other rapper. Then the other rapper would try to talk bad about him to see who can put who down the most. The winner is always decided by crowd reaction and participation. That's a battle.

Beatbox
Making a cappella bass and scratching sounds.

Chillin'
Chillin' is laid back and relaxed. As Ice says in his act, "This is Vanilla Ice, chillin' like Bob

Dylan, and maxin' like Michael Jackson, the VIP's got all the action.''

Cold
Cold means a freeze, ice, cold, and "cooler than ever." You can use cold in a phrase like, "Man that is cool," or "Man that is cold." Basically, it's just another word for cool.

Cold kickin' it
Cold kickin' it means you're "livin' large"—bigger than life.

Chump
A chump is a guy whom you would address as "Yo, Chump." A chump is basically the same as a punk.

Def
Def means the same thing as "dope." It's another word for "cool," as in "very cool."

Dis
Dis is to "disrespect."

Dope
It's the same as "def"—it's "cool to the extreme."

Extreme
Extreme is "takin' it to the max."

Fly
Fly is very cool. A person can also be a "flyguy" or a "flygirl." If you're "fly," you're hot and definitely going places.

Fresh
Fresh is just like it says: "you're fresh," "you're happenin'," "you're fresh on the box." Rhymers say, "You're fresh!" It's just another term for being cool.

Frontin'
Frontin' means: "you're frontin' somebody." The same thing as "dissin' somebody." Frontin' is simply another word for "dissin'."

Gauge
Gauge as in "12 gauge" [shotgun].

Hang
Hang means the same as "chillin'." Synonyms include "sittin' back relaxin'," "kickin' it with your homies."

Homies
Your close friends who you hang out with all the time are your homies. You can also say, "homeboys" or "homegirls."

Hottie'

A "hottie' " is a sexy girl.

Ice

As in "smooth as ice."

Illin'

Illin' is used in phrases like, "you be illin' ": "ill" as in "you're ill," "you're no-good."

Livin' large

Livin' large is like, "living like Michael Jackson," or "livin' like a star."

Mackin'

Mackin' is when you're "pulling" the girls. "Mackin' the women," means you're attracting all the women.

Maxin'

Maxin' is just like it says, "you're maxin'," "you're at your max," or "you're to the max."

Poppin' it

Poppin' as in "I'm poppin' it the most." "You're workin' it," "you're poppin' it."

Posse

Your posse is your crew, your buddies, the group you hang out with.

Profilin'
Profilin' is the same as showing off.

Rockin' the House
You're "tearin' the roof off the joint" when you're "rockin' the house."

Schemin'
Schemin' as in "to scheme." Also, "schemin' on a girl," which means that you're acting a certain way to attract a girl.

Slammin'
Slammin' means "kicking butt." Also, it's "dope."

Word to Your Mother
Ice has two definitions for this one. (1) Originally it was the phrase "word to the mother" on the street. But when Ice says it, he says "word to *your* mother." All of the black artists say "word to the mother," and in that context, "mother" refers to "motherland." The sentiment is, let's all live together. "Word to your mother," on the other hand, means "always listen to your mother."

Yo
Yo means, "check this out."

THE VANILLA ICE POSSE

What's a rapper without his posse? Totally lost in the not-so-cool world of "alone." Vanilla Ice is very tight with his group of homies on the road with him, and the entire cast and crew involved with Ice's music and with his show are more like a family than a mere working unit of performers and technicians. According to the members of the group, they all enjoy each other's company, and whether they're on a plane, onstage, or back at the hotel maxin' and relaxin', they're always there for each other. Here's a rundown on each of them.

High Tech has been with the Vanilla Ice Posse the longest—about three years. His real name is John Huffman. Ice has believed in High Tech from the beginning, even though others doubted his talent. He could spot the makings of a good dancer, and his instinctive belief in High Tech never wavered. Ice has a lot of good things to say about High Tech's persistence. He says that although at first High Tech didn't even know how to dance at all ("I mean—not one lick!"), he stuck with it through all of the tough times, and rehearsed a lot. "He had the rhythm, but I just steadily taught him the moves and stuff," Ice says. But since High Tech worked so hard, he's now one of Ice's best dancers. High Tech lives in Dallas, but he's originally from Vacaville, California, which is between Oakland and Sacramento.

The other two dancers in the posse are Juice and E-Rock. Ice first saw them dancing at a club in Dallas in early 1990. At the time they were "100.3 dancers," named for the Dallas radio station 100.3. They knew who Ice was and when he asked them to come out on the road with the posse, there was no answer other than "Sure!" E-Rock's name is Everett Fitzgerald and Juice's name is Mark Grinage.

Ice would not be without these guys. As he explains it, "We're like a big family. We hang out together, and we do a lot of stuff." In fact, they spend most of their time together. They travel together on the road, often with a very tough schedule.

Earthquake is Ice's deejay. He co-wrote "Ice Ice Baby" and "Play That Funky Music," and he's featured on the whole album. Earthquake's real name is Floyd Brown, and he was at the City Lights club when it all started.

When on the road, Ice travels with his stage manager, Tony-T; his road manager, John Bush; and his sound tech, Allen Laws, who sets up all of the equipment and makes sure that everything is in place. Tony-T tapes the floor—so Ice and his posse will know where to be during the performance. He hooks up all of the equipment, carries it from the truck, and takes care of the banners and the backdrops. Deejay D/Dope Deshay is no longer with the posse. Of his absence, Ice has stated: "He was a great deejay, and we had some good times together as well. I have nothing bad to say about him—no hard feelings at all."

Ice recalls the day when "Ice Ice Baby" hit Number One as the greatest day of his life. Reminiscing, Ice has explained, "I had a party, and everything was great. It was like a dream come true for me. I never thought it would happen." When "To the Extreme" went to Number One, his mind was totally blown. "I was like, 'Oh, my God—I've got the top album in the country!' I was going, 'Oh, my God—I cannot believe this! This is great!' "

There are two other members of the posse that are especially close to Ice—his security guards, Big E and Chilly. To Ice, Big E and Chilly are much more than employees, they are his homies, and they hang out with him. They were shown with Ice in *People* magazine recently. They're known in the business as great security guards who are really cool tempered.

Ice and his posse have had some good times together at charity events. On August 30, 1990, Ice and his posse played basketball with some deejays from station WAGH-FM in Columbus, Georgia, for a benefit for the Jordan High Band Booster Club. As Ice explains, it wasn't exactly what they expected. He says that instead of a team of deejays, the opposing team had two deejays and other guys who were playing college basketball. But Ice and his team stuck with them, losing by only one point.

VANILLA ICE'S DEF FAVORITES

If you really want to get to know someone, simply find out his favorite things. Here are some of the fascinating facts about the legendary Iceman:

Ice's favorite food?
Pizza
If he were ordering a pizza, what would he order on it?
Triple pepperoni and double cheese
What's his favorite pizza place in New York?
John's Pizza
What's his favorite pizza place in Miami?
Pizzeria Uno
What's his favorite pizza place in Dallas?

Campisi's/The Egyptian

What are his favorite TV shows?

Fresh Prince of Bel-Air, *21 Jump Street*, and *Miami Vice*

Who is his favorite movie actor?

Morgan Freeman. According to Ice: "He's got to be the best actor in the world. He is so good, he makes it look real. He is a great actor."

Who is his favorite actress?

Kim Basinger.

What is his favorite car?

Says Ice: "I just got a brand new car, an Acura NSX. They only made 1,500 of these cars. It's the only white one in history with white leather and white wheels." The car is similar in appearance to a Ferrari Testarossa but it is more rounded and sleeker.

What's his favorite color?

"White and black are my favorite two colors and I like to see them used together," he proclaims. "On black, white shines the most; and on white, black shines the most."

What's his favorite holiday?

Halloween!

What's his favorite sport?

Motocross

Does he believe in astrology?

Yes. "I'm a Scorpio. I didn't believe in it

until a girlfriend of mine read my horoscope and it came true."

What are his favorite places in New York City?

John's Pizza, Times Square, the Village, and shopping at Unique Clothing Warehouse. "They had some really cool airbrushed designs on jackets there."

What is his favorite basketball team?

The Phoenix Suns

What is his favorite football team?

The Miami Dolphins

What is his favorite baseball team?

"I don't get into baseball," he says.

Vanilla Ice's Top Ten Favorite Movies

When Vanilla Ice is hangin' with his homies, and it's time to rent a video, here's what you'll be likely to find on his television screen:

1. *The Abyss*
2. *Ghost*
3. *The Exorcist*
4. *Less Than Zero*
5. *Colors*
6. *Breakin'*
7. *On Any Sunday*

8. *Speedway*
9. *Flatliners*
10. *Predator*

Vanilla Ice's Top Ten Favorite Singing Stars

If you were to go with Vanilla Ice to your favorite record store, here are the stars that you would find him checking out:

1. 2 Live Crew
2. Eric B. & Rakim
3. Big Daddy Kane
4. James Brown
5. Steve Miller
6. UB40
7. Queen Latifah
8. Salt 'n' Pepa
9. Run DMC
10. Whodini

ICE ON ICE

In spite of Ice's minor press faux pas that he made with concealing his real name and the silly mix-up over which high school he attended, the fact remains that he is sharp, talented, and handsome. There may be disputes about his alma mater, but it doesn't diminish his ability to make music, sell records, and dazzle crowds from Los Angeles to London with his rappin' and dancin'.

I especially began following his exploits while he was on the M. C. Hammer tour. From the start, I was drawn to his "rap & roll" way of expressing his own personal feelings about life, music, and the pursuit of a seriously slammin' time.

In addition to his love of performing, Ice also loves the recording process of going into the studio. And he says he's learning a lot about the recording process, too. He shares mixing credits for "Ice Ice Baby" and "Funky Music" with Paul Loomis. He even said that he can see himself producing other artists. It's just a matter of finding out what the rapper or singer likes. He sees himself one day producing somebody big, and he would also like to help make someone unknown into a big star as well. It's his dream to "discover" somebody that nobody knows about and produce his debut disc.

Ice writes his raps whenever he's inspired to do so, even if he's on the road. He has come up with a few cuts already. In concert recently, he previewed five or six new songs. He has plans to cut three or four of them for his next album, which he has been working on. He performs some of the new songs live, interspersing preview segments of them in the show each night, just to see what the crowd's reaction will be. He has a song he has written called "Vanilla Ice to the Extreme," and the crowd reaction has been fantastic, so he's been performing it more and more in the show.

When Ice was on the *Arsenio Hall* show, he didn't have much time for an interview or to perform more than once because he had a live show to do later that night. Arsenio's audience went crazy over his performance, and he had a great time. Ice also did *Club MTV* with Downtown Julie Brown, who, says Ice, "is very sexy."

Ice has also spoken on the subject of drugs. If a friend of his were having trouble with drugs, he has continually claimed that he would try to help him or her out any way he could. If that didn't work, he'd try his best just to talk the friend out of it, whether the friend wanted to listen or not. "I'd definitely tell them to stay off of it, and be cool," Ice says. "It can ruin your life, it can kill you."

As for his career, Ice is reaching for the top. He'd like to have more than just one, two, or three number one records. Ice's future may find him emerging as one of rap music's premier leaders. In other words, one of the biggest rappers of all times.

Despite his popularity, Ice still feels that the press should treat him more fairly. He has discovered that he appreciates Europe almost as much as New York City. The group traveled to London, England, and to Munich, Stuttgart, and Bremen, Germany. "The food wasn't too good, but everything else was cool," he reported in the media. It was his first visit to a non-English-speaking country, and he got a big charge out of it.

Although Ice didn't have time to be a real tourist, he did get to do several radio, print, and television interviews. Ice appeared on *Eurotops* in Germany, and *Smash Hits* in London. *Smash Hits* is hosted by Jason Donovan, who's a very popular TV host over there.

What are Ice's fans like? "I don't want to tell," he has explained in interviews with the press. "It would sound like I'm bragging." But just watch his live shows and you'll see the reaction. In his stage show he says to his audience, "How's this side over here, the left side?" The audience always begins screaming. Then he asks, "How does the middle feel?" And they also scream. Then he asks the right side of the crowd, and they too go crazy. When he says, "Yo ladies, are you with me?" all of the girls really scream—loud! Then Ice raises his right hand and asks all the ladies in the house to say "Go Ice! Go!" and they shout it extra loud. When he says "Yo fellas," all of the fellas do a howl. They're loud, but the ladies just overwhelm them. About seventy percent of the people at his autograph signings are female, Vanilla estimates, making him feel like quite the ladies' man.

He enjoys his success, but recognizes its downside, too. At the MTV Awards show in September, Ice got to meet a lot of his favorite performers. "Everybody who was anybody was there," he boasted. "Young MC came up to me and said, 'Yo, you're Vanilla Ice, right?' and I said, 'Yeah.' And he said, 'Congratulations, you've got a slammin' album, man!'" He took that comment as a great compliment, because he digs Young MC, and found him to be a very nice guy. He didn't get to meet Madonna, because she spent a lot of time backstage. However, he thought her act was great. He especially liked the choreography. "My favorite performer that night was Janet Jackson—she tore it up! She took it all at the MTV Awards!" She was the very first act to perform that night, and according to Ice, nobody topped her for the rest of the evening.

Ice doesn't have a girlfriend at the moment, but he explains, "I had a girlfriend for about three years, but it didn't work out because I was gone all the time. So, I'm single at the moment. But if a girl catches my eye . . ."

So who *is* Vanilla Ice, what is it that makes his rap unique, and how do Ice and his music fit into the bigger picture of rock and roll? Now that he is an international recording star, is his legend fact or fiction? And will his career and his fame last? No one is quite sure—or more truthfully, it's simply too soon to tell. I've reviewed the facts, and tried to piece together who Vanilla Ice is and what he stands for, yet the question remains, "Does he represent the next wave of popular music, or is his music simply a synthesis of everything that has come before him?" Only time will tell. Rap is legitimately recognized as the perfect medium in which to mix elements of R&B, rock, soul, and funk. Because of Vanilla Ice's versatile rap album "To the Extreme," I predict that the sound of rap will continue to have a wider scope and a broader appeal.

And so continues the instant success story of Vanilla Ice. Whether he's "maxin' and relaxin'," "mackin' and schemin'," or "chillin' with his homies," you can be assured that Ice is going to spend the nineties perpetually workin' it. He's already recovered from the world finding out his true identity. Now that the "mystery man" facade has come down, he can just concentrate on his rapping and his budding movie career. This is not the end of the saga of the Iceman; in fact, it is just the dawn of the new ice age. Rest assured, homies, as far as exposing his talents, what we've heard from Vanilla Ice—is just the tip of the iceberg!

THE VANILLA ICE DISCOGRAPHY

ALBUMS:
(1) "Hooked" Ultrax Records (1990)
(2) "To the Extreme" SBK/Ultrax Records (1990)

SINGLES:
(1) "Play That Funky Music"/"Ice Ice Baby" Ultrax Records (1990)
(2) "Ice Ice Baby" SBK/Ultrax Records (1990)
(3) "Play That Funky Music" SBK/Ultrax Records (1990)

(4) "Stop That Train" SBK/Ultrax Records (1991)

VIDEOS:

(1) "Ice Ice Baby" SBK/Ultrax Records (1990)

(2) "Play That Funky Music" SBK/Ultrax Records (1990)

(3) "Stop That Train" SBK/Ultrax Records (1990)

BIBLIOGRAPHY

Information for this book has previously appeared on the pages of the following publications:

Billboard
Time
Newsweek
U.S.A. Today
Spin
Dallas Morning News
Miami Herald
Teen Machine
Teen Dreams
Music Connection

People
Dallas Times Herald
New York *Daily News*
New York Times
Newsday
Ft. Worth *Star Telegram*
Los Angeles Times
Hits

ABOUT THE AUTHOR

MARK BEGO is the author of several best-selling books on rock & roll and show business. He recently published his collaboration with singing star Debbie Gibson, entitled *Between the Lines* (1989), and the biography *Linda Ronstadt: It's So Easy* (1990). Bego has been heralded in the press as "The Prince of Pop Music Bios." His other books include *Aretha Franklin: The Queen of Soul* (1989), *Bette Midler: Outrageously Divine* (1987), *Cher!* (1986), *Whitney!* [Houston] (1986), *Julian Lennon!* (1986), *Sade!* (1986), *Madonna!* (1985), *On the Road with Michael!* [Jackson] (1984), *The Doobie Brothers* (1980), *Barry Manilow* (1977), and *The Captain*

& *Tennille* (1977). His Michael Jackson biography, *Michael!* (1984), spent six weeks on *The New York Times* Best-Seller List, and sold over three million copies in six different languages.

Bego's books have also encompassed several other entertainment industry subjects. He has written about television: *TV Rock: The History of Rock & Roll on Television* (1988) and *The Linda Gray Story* (1988)—and the movies: *The Best of Modern Screen* (1986) and *Rock Hudson: Public & Private* (1986).

His writing has appeared in several magazines and newspapers including *People, Us, The Star, Celebrity, Cosmopolitan, Penthouse, The Music Connection, Billboard,* and *The National Enquirer.* For two years Bego was the editor in chief of *Modern Screen* magazine, and he frequently appears on radio and television, talking about the lives and careers of the stars. Mark Bego divides his time between New York City, Los Angeles, and Tucson, Arizona.